Built for Speed

The World's Fastest Military Airplanes

by Michael Burgan

Consultant:
Raymond L. Puffer, Ph.D.
Historian
Edwards AFB History Office

CAPSTONE BOOKS
an imprint of Capstone Press
Mankato, Minnesota

Capstone Books are published by Capstone Press
151 Good Counsel Drive, P.O. Box 669, Mankato, Minnesota 56002
http://www.capstone-press.com

Library of Congress Cataloging-in-Publication Data
Burgan, Michael.
    The world's fastest military airplanes/by Michael Burgan.
    p. cm.—(Built for speed)
    Includes bibliographical references and index.
    Summary: Explains how jet planes operate and some of the uses that the military
makes of them, describing the design and functioning of such examples as the F-15,
the AV-8B Harrier, and the F-22 stealth plane.
    ISBN 0-7368-0568-0
    1. Airplanes, Military—Juvenile literature. [1. Jet planes. 2. Airplanes, Military.]
I. Title. II. Series.
UG1240 .B87 2001
623.7'46—dc21   00-023086

Editorial Credits
Carrie A. Braulick, editor; Timothy Halldin, cover designer and illustrator; Erin Scott,
    Sarin Creative, illustrator; Katy Kudela, photo researcher

Photo Credits
Defense Visual Information Center, 4, 10, 20, 26, 30, 35, 38 (top, bottom), 39 (top)
Edwards AFB History Office, cover, 32, 39 (bottom)
Index Stock Imagery, 29
International Stock/Maratea, 12
Mark Reinstein/Pictor, 15, 36
Matt Swinden, 17 (top, bottom)
NASA, 40, 42
Unicorn Stock Photos/Marshall Prescott, 23
Visuals Unlimited/Corinne Humphrey, 8; Steve Strickland, 24
William B. Folsom, 19

  2 3 4 5 6 06 05 04 03 02

Table of Contents

Chapter 1

Fast Military Airplanes

The world's fastest aircraft are military planes. These planes have many uses. Some military planes are used in battles. Fast military planes can quickly reach enemy targets. Their speed also helps them avoid being shot down by enemy planes.

Military forces also use fast planes for reconnaissance missions. A plane's crew watches an enemy's actions during these missions. Reconnaissance planes usually fly high above the ground. This altitude makes it difficult for enemies to detect these planes.

Some military forces build experimental planes. Engineers test new ideas as they make

Military forces often use fast military planes during battles.

these planes. Experimental planes are not used in battles. But these planes may help engineers build even faster planes in the future.

Jet Engines

Jet engines power most of the fastest military planes. Planes that use jet engines often are called jets.

Jet engines suck in air. A device called a compressor presses the air together. This compressed air is mixed with fuel and ignited. The mixture then burns while planes fly.

Fuel that burns inside jet engines creates hot gases. The temperature of these gases is more than 2,000 degrees Fahrenheit (1,100 degrees Celsius). The gases rush out the rear of the engines and travel at a speed of nearly 1,700 feet (500 meters) per second. The force of the moving gases pushes planes forward.

Some jet engines have an afterburner. This device burns extra fuel to create more power for planes. It is located near the rear of the engine.

Different types of jet engines exist. These include turbojet and turbofan engines. Most military planes use turbofan engines. Turbojet

TURBOFAN ENGINE

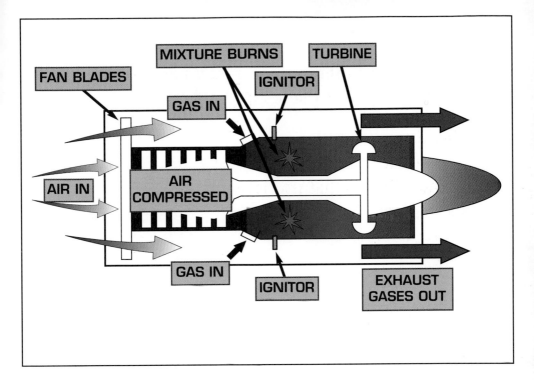

FAN BLADES

MIXTURE BURNS

TURBINE

IGNITOR

GAS IN

AIR IN

AIR COMPRESSED

GAS IN

IGNITOR

EXHAUST GASES OUT

and turbofan engines work similarly. Both have a fan to suck in air. A device called a turbine keeps the fan operating. But turbofan engines suck in more air and burn less fuel than turbojet engines.

Military planes may use jet engines called ramjets in the future. These engines do not contain a fan. The engines compress the air as the planes fly at high speeds. Planes with ramjets need another power source to help them

Workers often check jet engines to make sure they are operating properly.

reach high speeds. For example, a rocket booster may push the planes forward when they take off.

The Speed of Sound

The world's fastest planes fly faster than the speed of sound. Sound travels at about 760 miles (1,200 kilometers) per hour at sea level. This is the average level of the ocean's surface. The speed of sound changes depending on an object's altitude. It usually decreases as an object's altitude increases. The speed of sound is about 660 miles (1,100 kilometers) per hour at a height of 40,000 feet (12,192 meters).

Scientists label planes that fly faster than the speed of sound with a Mach number. Mach numbers are named after Ernst Mach. Mach was an Austrian scientist who studied the speed of sound. A plane flying at the speed of sound while at 40,000 feet (12,192 meters) has reached Mach 1.0. A plane flying at twice the speed of sound at the same altitude is flying at Mach 2.0.

Planes that fly at speeds between Mach 1.0 and Mach 5.0 are called supersonic jets. Planes that fly at or above Mach 5.0 are called hypersonic jets. Today, no military planes can reach Mach 5.0. Only one plane has flown faster than Mach 5.0. This plane was an experimental plane called the X-15. It reached Mach 6.7.

Planes create a loud booming noise when they reach Mach 1.0. This sound is called a sonic boom. Air piles up in front of a plane that travels faster than the speed of sound. This creates high air pressure. The pressure creates a shock wave. The shock wave turns into a sound wave as it travels

away from the plane. A sonic boom occurs when the sound wave hits the ground. A sonic boom often sounds like a clap of thunder.

Motion and Forces

Engineers design airplanes to overcome various forces. Gravity is one of these forces. Gravity pulls objects toward Earth's surface. Planes must create enough lift to overcome gravity. Lift is the force that pulls planes into the air. Planes use their wings and engine power to create lift.

Planes also must overcome drag. This force is created when air strikes a moving object. Drag slows down planes as they fly through the air. Engineers design planes with powerful engines to overcome drag. They also build aerodynamic planes. These planes are shaped to easily cut through the air. Engineers make aerodynamic planes with pointed front ends. They also may set the planes' wings back at an angle.

Powerful engines help airplanes create lift and overcome drag.

Chapter 2

The F-15 Eagle

The F-15 Eagle has a perfect air-combat record. F-15 pilots have earned more than 100 victories against enemy aircraft with no losses. F-15s are fighter jets. Fighter jets are designed to attack enemy planes in the air.

The U.S. military has more than 400 F-15s. The air forces of Japan, Israel, and Saudi Arabia also use these planes.

F-15s are one of the world's fastest fighter jets. They can fly as fast as 1,875 miles (3,017 kilometers) per hour. They reach Mach 2.8. Very few fighter jets can fly faster. F-15s also can quickly climb to high altitudes. They can travel from the ground to an altitude of 30,000 feet (9,144 meters) in less than 1 minute.

F-15s are designed to fly at high speeds and shoot down enemy forces in the air.

F-15s were effective during the Gulf War (1991). This war began when Iraq invaded Kuwait. The United States Air Force (USAF) helped force Iraq's military out of Kuwait. Nearly all of Iraq's air combat losses during the war were due to F-15s.

F-15 Models

Different models of F-15s exist. The first model flew in 1972. This plane is the F-15A. The F-15A is designed to carry only one person. The USAF soon flew F-15Bs. These planes are similar to F-15As. But F-15Bs can carry two people instead of one.

Today, the USAF uses three F-15 models. These are the F-15C, the F-15D, and the F-15E. F-15Cs carry one pilot. F-15Ds and F-15Es carry a pilot and one other crewmember. Both F-15Cs and F-15Ds carry more fuel than earlier models. This allows them to fly for longer periods of time without refueling. These planes also have a special radar device. Radar uses radio waves to find distant planes and objects. The F-15's radar allows pilots to track one target while searching for other targets at the same time.

The USAF often used F-15s to force Iraq's military out of Kuwait during the Gulf War.

All current F-15 models share several features. They have a heads-up display (HUD) in the cockpit. The HUD shows flight information. For example, pilots can see their current speed and the position of other planes near them. The HUD is located directly in front of the pilot. This allows pilots to look straight ahead at all times. In other planes, pilots sometimes must look down to see flight information. F-15s also have low wing loading. This means their wings are large compared to the planes' weight. Low wing loading allows F-15s to turn quickly.

F-15 engines have a high thrust-to-weight ratio. They produce a great deal of power compared to their weight. Thrust is the force that moves an airplane forward. A jet engine's thrust is measured in pounds. F-15s have two engines. Each F-15C or F-15D engine produces 23,450 pounds (10,637 kilograms) of thrust. Each F-15E engine produces 29,000 pounds (13,154 kilograms) of thrust. F-15s' high thrust-to-weight ratio allows them to gain speed quickly.

F-15Es have features not found in other F-15s. These planes fight air battles like other F-15s. But F-15Es also are designed to attack targets on the ground. These planes also have a forward-looking infra-red (FLIR) sensor. These sensors detect heat that is given off by objects. FLIR sensors allow

Safety in the Sky

Supersonic jets can be dangerous to fly. These planes need special safety features to protect their pilots. Pilots of most military planes strap

themselves into an ejection seat before they take off. Pilots use ejection seats if their planes are going to crash. Ejection seats have a parachute inside of them. These pieces of strong, light fabric allow pilots to land safely on the ground or in water. The pilots pull a handle that shoots the ejection seat out of the plane. The parachute opens when the seat falls away.

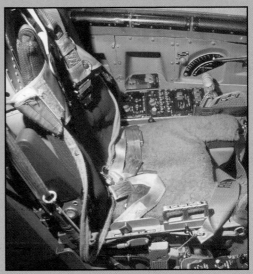

Crewmembers of supersonic

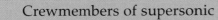

jets also wear G-suits. These suits protect crewmembers from the force

of gravity. The force of gravity on a person standing on flat ground is called 1 g. G forces can increase and decrease as objects gain speed and slow down. For example, a plane's sudden burst of speed raises the force of gravity. Crewmembers may experience a g force of 8 during parts of a flight. At these times, their bodies seem to be eight times heavier. This high g force creates strong pressure. The pressure can damage people's bodies. Blood may collect in the lower parts of crewmembers' bodies and cause them to become unconscious. G-suits are filled with air. They put pressure on the lower parts of crewmembers' bodies to prevent blood from collecting in these areas.

F-15 crewmembers to see targets at night or during bad weather conditions. F-15Es flew at night and destroyed Iraqi missile sites during the Gulf War.

F-15s in Battle

F-15s perform well during dogfights. Planes try to shoot each other down during these mid-air battles. F-15s can turn and dive while flying at high speeds. These moves help pilots avoid being shot down by enemy planes.

F-15 crewmembers can use a variety of weapons. They may fire missiles. These explosives can travel long distances. F-15s use different kinds of missiles. These include AIM-7F Sparrows and AIM-9L Sidewinders. Crewmembers usually fire Sparrow missiles at night and in bad weather conditions. They fire Sidewinder missiles during the day and in clear weather conditions. Crewmembers also may fire bullets from an M-61A1 cannon.

F-15Es are designed to fly at night and during bad weather conditions.

F-15E pilots often perform interdiction missions. Pilots continuously attack enemy positions during these missions. F-15E pilots often encounter heavy enemy fire during interdiction missions.

Chapter 3

The SR-71A Blackbird

The SR-71A Blackbird is the world's fastest plane. Blackbirds are reconnaissance jets. Their top speed is about 2,190 miles (3,500 kilometers) per hour. They can reach Mach 3.2. Blackbirds can fly at Mach 3.0 for more than an hour at a time.

Blackbirds also can fly higher than any other planes. Their ceiling is slightly higher than 85,000 feet (25,908 meters). A plane's ceiling is the highest altitude it can reach.

Designed for Spying

USAF pilots first flew Blackbirds in 1962. In February 1964, the U.S. government announced

Blackbirds are the world's fastest military planes.

that Blackbirds existed. Before this time, the planes were classified. Classified information is secret.

Blackbirds are similar to reconnaissance planes called A-12s. The military once used these planes to take pictures of enemy territory. But A-12s needed to fly directly over the land to take pictures. Blackbirds use special cameras that take pictures from a distance. They do not need to fly into enemy territory. This helped Blackbirds become the U.S. military's best spy planes.

The high speed and altitude capabilities of Blackbirds allow them to perform reconnaissance missions safely. Blackbirds are not equipped with weapons. Planes flying at high speeds are difficult to shoot down. No Blackbirds have been shot down during reconnaissance missions.

Many features help Blackbirds fly at high speeds. Blackbirds have an aerodynamic shape to reduce drag. Their front end is long and pointed. Their wings are shaped like triangles. Blackbirds are made almost entirely of a strong

Blackbirds have a pointed front end and triangular wings to reduce drag.

metal called titanium. This metal resists the heat that Blackbirds create at high speeds.

Blackbirds have two powerful engines. Each engine has a thrust of 32,500 pounds (14,742 kilograms). The Blackbird's afterburner can run longer than those of most other military planes.

In 1990, the USAF stopped using Blackbirds. The U.S. government did not supply the USAF with money to continue

Two powerful jet engines with afterburners help Blackbirds fly at supersonic speeds.

using the planes. The government believed satellites in space could take better pictures of enemy actions. Satellites are communication objects that orbit Earth.

The USAF began using Blackbirds again in 1994. These Blackbirds have improvements. They have more powerful cameras and communication systems. But the U.S.

government again discontinued the Blackbird program in 1998.

Other Missions and Uses

Blackbirds sometimes flew missions that were not related to reconnaissance. People used them for search-and-rescue missions after natural disasters. In 1980, the U.S. military used a Blackbird to inspect damage caused by the eruption of Mount Saint Helens. This volcano eruption in Washington state killed 57 people. Crewmembers in the Blackbird looked for survivors. Blackbirds also were used to find crashed planes.

Today, the National Aeronautics and Space Administration (NASA) uses Blackbirds for research. NASA is in charge of the U.S. space program. It uses two Blackbirds to test ideas for building hypersonic jets. The USAF may use hypersonic planes in the future.

Chapter 4

The AV-8B Harrier

The AV-8B Harrier is one of the world's most unusual military planes. These planes are vertical or short takeoff and landing (V/STOL) planes. Harriers can take off and land on runways as most planes do. But Harriers also can take off and land vertically as helicopters do. Harriers sometimes are called "jumpjets."

Harriers have a top speed of 629 miles (1,012 kilometers) per hour. These planes are transonic. They fly just below supersonic speeds. Other planes can fly faster than Harriers. But Harriers can quickly reach high altitudes. Harriers can travel from the ground to 40,000 feet (12,192 meters) in about 2 minutes.

Harriers can quickly climb to high altitudes.

Harrier Design

The Royal Air Force of Great Britain first flew Harriers in 1964. The British called them Kestrel FGA1s. The U.S. Marine Corps flew an early model of the Harrier in 1970. The USAF called these planes AV-8As. Today, Marine Corps members often fly Harriers. Military pilots in Italy and Spain also fly these planes.

Airplane manufacturers built two improved Harrier models for the U.S. military. These are the Harrier AV-8B II and the Harrier AV-8B II Plus. These planes have larger wings, stronger landing gear, and more powerful engines than earlier models. The Harrier AV-8B II Plus also has a special radar system to help pilots locate objects at night.

Harriers' wing design helps increase lift as the planes begin to fly into the air. The wings are broader than the wings of most military planes. They also are rounded at the edges. But these wings increase drag. This decreases Harriers' speed capability.

Harriers' wings are broad and rounded.

Harriers sometimes carry bombs underneath their wings.

Engine Nozzles

Harriers have one turbofan engine. Nozzles on this engine help the planes perform vertical takeoffs and landings. These round pieces of metal direct the engine's exhaust. Harrier pilots point the nozzles down for vertical takeoffs. The force of the exhaust through the nozzles pushes the planes up. Pilots then point the nozzles straight back. This causes the exhaust gases to push the planes forward.

Pilots can point the nozzles in different directions to change position during dogfights. This allows pilots to move into a favorable firing position or avoid being shot down.

Harriers in Battle

Harriers are useful on missions. Most jets need runways to take off and land. But Harriers can take off from almost any flat surface. They may take off from concrete pads. Harriers often arrive at mission sites sooner than other planes because they can remain near battle areas. During the Gulf War, a group of Harrier planes operated from a ship in the Persian Gulf. This large body of water borders Iraq and Kuwait.

Harriers are used mainly for ground attacks. They can fire small rockets or missiles at ground targets. Harriers sometimes carry bombs. These bombs may weigh as much as 1,000 pounds (454 kilograms). Some of these bombs are called "smart" bombs. Beams of light called lasers guide these bombs to their targets. Harriers also may carry cluster bombs. These bombs release small explosives called bomblets. The bomblets are designed to hit enemy soldiers on the ground.

Chapter 5

The F-22 Raptor

The USAF is currently testing a new supersonic fighter plane. This plane is the F-22 Raptor. The USAF plans to replace F-15 Eagles with F-22 Raptors.

The USAF currently flies F-22 test models. F-22s fly at speeds greater than Mach 2.0. Their top speed is about 1,450 miles (2,300 kilometers) per hour. Their ceiling is about 65,000 feet (19,800 meters).

Designed for Stealth

F-22s are the world's fastest stealth planes. These planes are hard to spot using radar. Radar waves bounce off most planes and return to the radio antenna that sent them. This allows radar to give the location of the planes.

F-22s are the world's fastest stealth planes.

F-22s have features that make them difficult to detect by radar. The outside parts of F-22s have many angles. Radar waves hit the angled parts. The waves then shoot out in many directions instead of bouncing back. F-22s also carry weapons inside storage areas called bays. Planes that carry weapons internally have fewer surfaces that radar can locate.

F-22s in Battle

F-22s have several advantages during battles. They have special computer systems. These computers collect information about what is happening both inside and outside of the planes. The computers then combine the information and display it on screens. This helps pilots keep track of what is happening on the battlefield.

Computers in F-22s perform other tasks. An F-22 pilot can see the computer information from another F-22 flying nearby. F-22 computers also can receive information from planes called E-3 Sentrys. These planes search for enemy aircraft. Information from other planes allows pilots to rely less on radios for

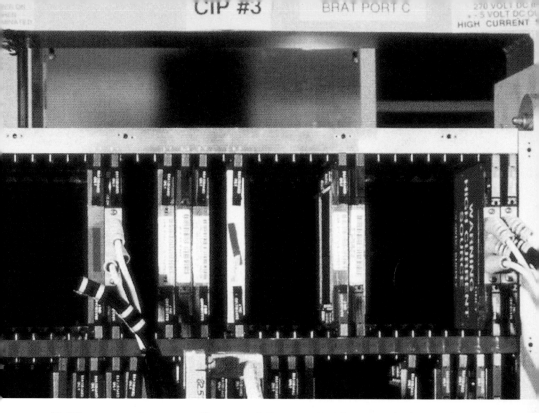

F-22 computers are the world's most advanced on-board flight computers.

communication. They then can concentrate on fighting enemies.

F-22s have advanced engines. These engines allow F-22s to supercruise. This means F-22s can fly at supersonic speeds for long time periods without using afterburners. F-22s save fuel as they supercruise. F-22 engines also have nozzles similar to those on Harriers. F-22 pilots move these nozzles to change the direction of

Airplane manufacturers spent a great deal of time designing and testing the YF-22.

the exhaust gases. This helps F-22s turn quickly to avoid being hit by enemy weapons.

F-22s carry up to eight missiles during combat. They also carry a cannon. F-22 crewmembers use these weapons to shoot down other planes.

Testing F-22s

New jets take many years to design and build. The USAF decided to replace F-15s in 1981.

Manufacturers completed the first F-22 prototype in 1990. This test model was called the YF-22.

F-22 manufacturers performed tests to make sure they were designing the plane properly. They put models of the plane into wind tunnels. The air in wind tunnels moves at high speeds. Wind tunnels show how a plane will fly in the air.

In 1991, the USAF approved the YF-22 prototype. The USAF then began in-flight tests with the prototype. They made sure the YF-22 could complete in-flight refueling. Another plane supplies fuel to the YF-22 in mid-air during this process. The USAF also made sure the YF-22 could reach supersonic speeds.

The first production F-22 flew in 1997. Production planes are final models. Nine F-22s currently are available for flight testing. The USAF plans to continue testing these planes until about 2003.

FAST FACTS

THE F-15 EAGLE

Built By: McDonnell Douglas
First Flown: 1972
Engines: Two turbofans with
         afterburners
Length: 63.8 feet (19.4 meters)
Height: 18.5 feet (5.6 meters)
Wingspan: 42.8 feet (13 meters)
Weight (empty): 27,000 pounds
              (12,247 kilograms)
Ceiling: 65,000 feet
      (19,812 meters)
Top Speed: 1,875 miles (3,017
         kilometers) per
         hour/Mach 2.8

THE SR-71A BLACKBIRD

Built By: Lockheed-Martin
First Flown: 1964
Engines: Two turbojets with
         afterburners
Length: 107.5 feet (32.7 meters)
Height: 18.6 feet (5.7 meters)
Wingspan: 55.7 feet (17 meters)
Weight (empty): 60,000 pounds
              (27,216 kilograms)
Ceiling: 85,000 feet
      (25,908 meters)
Top Speed: About 2,190 miles
         (3,500 kilometers) per
         hour/Mach 3.2

THE AV-8B HARRIER

Built By: McDonnell Douglas/Boeing
First Flown: 1978
Engines: One turbofan
Length: 46.4 feet (14.1 meters)
Height: 11.7 feet (3.6 meters)
Wingspan: 30.4 feet (9.3 meters)
Weight (empty): 12,500 pounds
              (5,670 kilograms)
Ceiling: 50,000 feet
       (15,240 meters)
Top Speed: 629 miles (1,012
          kilometers) per
          hour/Near Mach 1.0

THE F-22 RAPTOR

Built By: Lockheed-Martin and
          McDonnell Douglas/Boeing
First Flown: 1997
Engines: Two turbofans with
          afterburners
Length: 62.1 feet (19 meters)
Height: 16.5 feet (5 meters)
Wingspan: 44.6 feet (13.6 meters)
Weight (empty): 58,000 pounds
              (26,309 kilograms)
Ceiling: About 65,000 feet
       (19,800 meters)
Top Speed: About 1,450 miles
          (2,300 kilometers) per
          hour/Mach 2.2

Chapter 6

The Future of Military Planes

Engineers throughout the world continue to improve military planes. They work to improve jet engines. They also try to design planes with less drag. These efforts may create even faster military planes.

Faster Fighters

The USAF and F-22 manufacturers will continue to build and test F-22s. The United States plans to produce these planes until 2013. The USAF will probably fly F-22s for many years after that time.

Other countries also are building faster military planes. Military experts say the

NASA is currently working on Hyper-X. This plane may reach Mach 10.0.

The Hyper-X uses a rocket booster to help it reach high speeds.

Russian military is working on stealth fighters similar to F-22s. These planes are called SU-35s.

Hyper-X

Engineers also build experimental planes. They use these planes to test new ideas for future military planes. NASA is working on a plane called the X-43. This plane also is called Hyper-X. Engineers plan to make the Hyper-X hypersonic. It may fly as fast as Mach 10.0. This speed is more than 6,000 miles (9,700 kilometers) per hour. Flight tests on the Hyper-X began in 2000.

The Hyper-X uses a new kind of jet engine. These engines are called scramjets. Scramjets are similar to ramjets. But ramjets slow down the air after it enters the engine. The air in scramjet engines continues to move at a supersonic speed. This will help the Hyper-X reach faster speeds than planes with ramjets. Engineers may learn how to improve scramjets as they test the Hyper-X. Military planes with scramjets may be the world's fastest planes in the future.

Words to Know

afterburner (AF-tur-bur-nur)—the part of a jet engine that burns extra fuel to create more power

dogfight (DAWG-fite)—a mid-air battle between fighter planes

hypersonic (hye-pur-SON-ik)—a speed at or greater than Mach 5.0

lift (LIFT)—an upward force created by an airplane to overcome gravity

Mach (MAHK)—a unit of measurement for speeds faster than the speed of sound

radar (RAY-dar)—equipment that uses radio waves to locate distant objects

reconnaissance mission (ree-CAH-nuh-suhns MISH-uhn)—a mission to gather information about an enemy

supersonic (soo-pur-SON-ik)—a speed between Mach 1.0 and Mach 5.0

thrust (THRUHST)—the force that moves an airplane forward

To Learn More

Butterfield, Moira and Hans Jenssen. *Jets.* Look Inside Cross-Sections. New York: D K Publishing, 1996.

Graham, Ian. *Aircraft.* Built for Speed. Austin, Texas: Raintree Steck-Vaughn, 1999.

Green, Michael. *The United States Air Force.* Serving Your Country. Mankato, Minn.: Capstone Books, 1998.

Maynard, Christopher. *Aircraft.* The Need for Speed. Minneapolis: Lerner Publications, 1999.

Schleifer, Jay. *Fighter Planes.* Wings. Mankato, Minn.: Capstone Books, 1996.

Useful Addresses

Air Force Flight Test Center Museum
Edwards Air Force Base
Public Affairs
15 Yeager Boulevard
Edwards AFB, CA 93524

Canadian Museum of Flight
#200-5333 216th Street
Langley, BC V2Y 2N3
Canada

NASA Dryden Flight Research Center
P.O. Box 273
Edwards, CA 93523

National Air and Space Museum
Seventh and Independence Avenue SW
Washington, DC 20560

Internet Sites

Air Force Link
http://www.af.mil

Air Force Link Jr.
http://www.af.mil/aflinkjr/jr.htm

Airplane Pilots
http://militarycareers.com/occ/oairpil.htm

The Boeing Company
http://www.boeing.com/defense-space/
  military/military-site.html

Edwards Air Force Base
http://afftc.edwards.af.mil

F-22 Raptor
http://www.f-22raptor.com

Index